What Really Happens When You Die?

Ralph O. Muncaster

HARVEST HOUSE PUBLISHERS
Eugene, Oregon 97402

Cover by Terry Dugan Design, Minneapolis, Minnesota

By Ralph O. Muncaster

Are There Contradictions in The Bible?
Can Archaeology Prove the New Testament?
Can Archaeology Prove the Old Testament?
Can We Know for Certain We Are Going To Heaven?
Can You Trust The Bible?
Creation vs. Evolution
Does Prayer Really Work?
Does the Bible Predict the Future?
How Do We Know Jesus Is God?
How is Jesus Different from Other Religious Leaders?
How to Talk About Jesus With the Skeptics in Your Life
Is The Bible Really A Message From God?
Science - Was the Bible Ahead of It's Time?
What is the Proof For the Resurrection?
What is the Trinity?
What Really Happened Christmas Morning?
What Really Happens When You Die?
Why Are Scientists Turning to God?
Why Does God Allow Suffering?

WHAT REALLY HAPPENS WHEN YOU DIE?
Examine the Evidence Series

Copyright © 2000 by Ralph O. Muncaster
Published by Harvest House Publishers
Eugene, Oregon 97402

Library of Congress Cataloging-in-Publication Data

Muncaster, Ralph O.
     What really happens when you die? / Ralph O. Muncaster.
          p. cm. — (Examine the evidence series)
     Includes bibliographical references.
     ISBN 0-7369-0365-8
          1. Future life. I. Title.

BT902 .M86 2000
236'.2—dc21   00-039554

02 03 04 05 06 07 08 09 / BP / 10 9 8 7 6 5 4 3

Contents

Death . . .
Gruesome? Wonderful? Nothing?

Death lurks at everyone's doorstep. Perhaps it's 50 years away. Perhaps next year. Perhaps an hour from now.

Death is certain.

You have pondered death. Nearly everyone has—some with fear—some with wonder—most with uncertainty. Psychiatrists report that about 75 percent of all their patients are haunted or terribly disturbed at the prospect of death. The amazing thing is—

Few people *ever* actually investigate death.
Few attempt to understand death.
Few even talk about death.

Imagine knowing with certainty that a killer tornado would strike your neighborhood in the next few years. Wouldn't you learn all you could about tornados and what to do? Or imagine knowing with certainty that you would soon lose your job. If these events were *certain*, surely you would learn and prepare as much as you could. **Death *is* certain, unpredictable, unforgiving, and forever. *Learn all you can.***

Your preparation for death has
eternal consequences.

Regardless of your religious beliefs, there is a good chance that death is not the end of existence. In fact, there is *ample evidence* that life after death is a fact—as you will see in the following pages. Virtually all religious beliefs present some concept of what death means, and many provide guidance on how to have a "better afterlife."

So your *most important act in life* is to determine:

1. Is there life after death? (The answer will impact you forever.)

2. If so, which concept or idea is accurate?

3. What should you then do to enjoy eternity as much as possible?

These three questions will be answered in this book—which will also describe how to make death a *wonderful* experience.

The Key Issues

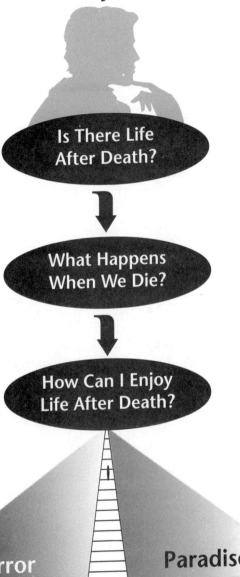

Is There Life After Death?

What Happens When We Die?

How Can I Enjoy Life After Death?

Horror

Paradise

FOREVER

FOREVER

Selecting the Guide to Life After Death

How do we know what to believe about life after death? Virtually all religions claim to speak with authority about the afterlife. The holy books of these religions are usually revered as authoritative sources.

How do we know which guide is accurate, if any?

Life after death is a supernatural event. It exists beyond time and space in a dimension we call the spirit world. God also exists in the spirit world. Therefore, if God has provided information about life after death through a holy writing, we might expect to find evidence that the writing itself is from beyond time and space.

How Do We Determine What Is from Beyond Time and Space?

"Miracle" is the word we use to describe something that is beyond our understanding, something that apparently has come from beyond time and space. We usually think of a miracle as an event. It might be a miraculous healing or some other event that seems to defy the laws of nature. So how do we detect miracles in the written words of a text thought to be authoritative?

Some religions claim that a holy book's beauty of language shows its divine inspiration (for example, Muslims claim this of the Qur'an). However, exceptional writers often demonstrate a similar skill. Other groups claim supernatural incidents of revelation as the basis for holy books (for example, the giving of the "miraculous" golden plates of the *Book of Mormon*). Yet no reasonable verification for these events exists.

The Bible displays several indicators of supernatural, miraculous inspiration. First, its *authorship* is amazing. Written by at least 40 authors of widely varying backgrounds over a period of 1500 years in various places, the Bible is constant and consistent on thousands of controversial topics.

Second, the Bible also has several kinds of *concealed evidence* embedded in its pages. Many models (or "types") and much numerical symbology, as well as similitudes and scientific insights, tie the centuries of biblical writings together.

And third, the Bible is miraculous in its *survival*. No other text has ever faced such intense efforts to obliterate it. Early Christians (and many even today) were killed merely for possessing a Bible. Most notably, in A.D. 303 an edict of the Roman emperor specified the death penalty for anyone found with a Bible. Countless Bibles were burned. Yet the Bible still survived. In fact, today we have more ancient copies of Bibles by far than of any other ancient text. Yet there is only one certain test of divine inspiration:

The only *sure* test of God's inspiration is—
perfect prediction of the future.

And the only way to verify the miracle of perfect prediction is to have contained in the text *historical* prophecies that can be confirmed later by the record of actual events. Predictions of end-time events are of no value in verifying the divine inspiration of a holy text *because they can never be tested*. Only specific prophecies of *historical* people, places, or events can confirm divine input.

Historical Prophecy in the Bible

The Bible is unique, in that it consistently foretells the future with absolute accuracy. Consider the fact that the Bible contains over 600 specific historical prophecies—with *not one* wrong. Most other holy books are totally void of historical prophecy. The test of anything being "from God" is prophecy (Deuteronomy 18:17-22; Isaiah 46:10). The Bible was written over a period of 1500 years;

we can trust the generations who came after the times of the prophecies for the historical facts, since they would have had no motive to conceal errors. These generations saw many specific historical events that confirmed the prophecies of the Bible.

Summary of the Accuracy of Biblical Prophecy[1]

	Old Testament Prophecies	New Testament Prophecies	Total	% of Total
Historically fulfilled	467	201	668	68%
Fulfillment not confirmed	2*	1*	3*	<1%
Heaven or the future (to be fulfilled)	105	237	342	32%
Total	574	439	1013	100%

Prophecy in Other Holy Books

The holy books of world religions contain virtually no verifiable historical prophecy. Some contain end-of-time prophecies that cannot be proven until the end of time—which does us no good as a test. Prophetic analysis of some of these holy books follows:

Failed Prophecies of Mormon Holy Books

The Book of Mormon—The following prophecy was written in 1823, long after Jesus was born: Jesus "shall be born . . . at Jerusalem" (Alma 7:10). He was actually born in Bethlehem. Some Mormons say Bethlehem was a part of Jerusalem, being only five miles away. Yet five miles at that time required more than an hour's travel—much like a 60-mile commute today. Even now, Bethlehem is considered a separate city from Jerusalem. This after-the-fact prophecy is false.

Doctrines and Covenants (D&C)—This book prophesied in 1832

* Prophecies whose fulfillment is not verified: Jeremiah 35:1-19; 49:1-6; John 1:49-51.

that a temple and a new Jerusalem would be built at a specific site in west Missouri within a generation (D&C 84:1-5,31). This was again emphasized in 1833 (D&C 97:19) and later (D&C 101:17-21)—that the new Jerusalem would *never* be moved from Missouri. Yet Salt Lake City became the "Jerusalem," and many generations have passed with no temple ever built in Missouri. These prophecies are false.

Failed Prophecies of the Jehovah's Witnesses

Various Publications—Many prophecies declaring the end of the world have been published by the Jehovah's Witnesses. The predictions mention these years: 1874 (*Studies in the Scriptures* 7:301); 1914 (same, 2:101) 1915; (same, 1914 edition); 1918 (same, 7:62); 1920 (same, 7:542); 1925 (*Millions Now Living Will Never Die*, Rutherford, 1920, page 97); 1942 (*The New World*, Rutherford, 1942, page 104); and 1975 (*Kingdom Ministry*, March 1968, page 4). Obviously, all such attempts at prophecy have failed.

Conclusion: The Bible is the *only* source with *100-percent prophetic accuracy*—and therefore is the only reliable authority on life after death.

What Is Life, and What Is Death?

To understand death, we first need to understand life. Why? Because death is *absence* of life. Similarly, it would be impossible to know about *lack* of wind without knowing about wind in the first place. The same could be said of electricity, gravity, and any number of things.

What Is Life?

Life has been defined strictly as "what living things do." For example, living things grow, reproduce, and respond to stimuli—and therefore are different from inanimate matter (Webster's dictionary). However, a nuclear explosion could also be said to grow, reproduce (by atomic chain reaction), and respond to stimuli. Yet no one would call it "life."

Why?

Life also involves things we absolutely cannot observe or even picture to ourselves, such as thought, emotions, planning, consciousness, creativity, and so on. Empirically,

- We cannot *measure* life. (We can only measure chemical, mechanical, and electrical responses.)

- We cannot *know* life. (We cannot know secret thoughts and emotions.)

- We cannot *create* life. (We cannot breathe life into dead or material things.)

- We definitely cannot be certain that anything can destroy life.

In summary:

- We do not really understand life.

- We cannot measure or know it. We cannot create it.

- We cannot see where life comes from. Nor can we see where life goes.

What Is Death?

Death is usually understood to be "the absence of life." And since we don't really know what life is, then we don't really know what death is—beyond our simple observation that typical "life functions" cease (that is, heartbeat, brainwaves, and so on). But does life itself cease? Or does it just move from one place to another, like heat escaping an oven?

Consider light. When you turn the lights off, is it "dead"? Does the light cease to exist? No. We can't see it anymore, and we can't measure it anymore. But someone in outer space with a very powerful telescope could at the right point in time. In fact, we now know that light travels very quickly in all directions and exists forever. Perhaps there is some parallel between light and life?

Some Physiological Considerations

Physiologists tell us that every non-skeletal cell in our body is replaced at most every seven years. Therefore, if life were simply matter or stored energy, it also would be replaced every seven years at most. Memory would be lost. Personalities would change. You would not be the same person.

Yet we know that this is not the case. We have memories of times past. We think about and feel things from the past. Our basic experiences and personality traits continue to define us as individuals. Obviously, the premise that life is nothing more than matter, chemistry, and electrical energy is far from the truth.

Intuition About Life After Death

Mankind has always perceived that there is life after death, as evidenced by many archaeological finds from virtually every culture. The Egyptians, for example, built pyramids as gigantic burial houses and employed detailed procedures for mummification—all to prepare people for the life beyond. American Indians placed corpses on wooden platforms to present people's spirits to the gods. Mankind has always honored the dead with special ceremonies (funerals).

Why are human beings the *only* creatures to memorialize the death of one of their kind, unlike animals, which at most simply bury carcasses? Perhaps the God of the universe designed human beings for a purpose or for a relationship with Him, which sets us apart from ordinary beasts. Perhaps this intuition is inborn in humans in the same way that instincts are born into all creatures.

Concepts of Life After Death

	Who is God?	What Happens at Death?	How to Attain Eternal Paradise
Hinduism	God is Brahman, a universal spirit that pervades everything.	Reincarnation to a status dependent on your present life.	Yoga and meditation. Can take many lifetimes.
Buddhism	Mostly atheistic. Buddha is God to some sects.	No soul or spirit. Your *beliefs* may be reincarnated.	No way to heaven. No soul or spirit.
Judaism	Orthodox— personal God. Other sects— impersonal.	Physical resurrection.	Be obedient and live with God.

	Who is God?	What Happens at Death?	How to Attain Eternal Paradise
Mormonism	Many gods. Elohim is god of the planet Earth. Man can become a god.	Most go to heaven. A few of the most evil go to darkness.	Work your way to godhood and heavenly levels by following Mormon rules.
Mind Sciences	An impersonal spirit. God is all. Jesus is just a man. Matter is illusion.	Death is not real. Sin, evil, and sickness are not real.	Not an issue, since everything is a state of mind, and there is no death.
Jehovah's Witnesses	Only Jehovah is God. Jesus is the first created being and will return to destroy non-JW's.	144,000 are already spirits in heaven. The rest live on earth 1000 years.	Must be baptized Jehovah's Witness and perfectly obey God during 1000 years to avoid annihilation.
New Age	God is essentially everything and everyone. God is impersonal.	Reincarnations until oneness with "God" is reached.	Offset bad karma with good karma. Meditate. Use occult practices.
Biblical Christianity	God is personal. God is One—the Father, Son (Jesus), and Holy Spirit (the Trinity).	Those who accept God's gift of Jesus go to heaven. Others go to Hades to await final judgment.	Believe and accept Jesus as Lord and Savior, who died for our sins, and rose again. Heaven is by grace, not by good works.

How Do We Know Life After Death Is Real?

What Is a Person?

We identify a physical body as a living person. But a body is just a "house" for the real person—the spirit. Our thoughts, our emotions, and our personality all reflect our spirit, which we can't see or measure. For instance, when someone's physical body becomes damaged beyond recognition—paralyzed, burned, or horribly deformed—we can almost always still identify that person by the manifestations of his personality, even though we can't recognize him by appearance.

Does our spirit die? The evidence suggests not. We continue to mature as a person until death. Even though our brain "storage system" might decline or be damaged, our experience and insight continue to grow—unlike our physical body, which deteriorates.

A body is made up of matter. It decays and dies. But our spirit is an intangible essence that grows and prospers. It only makes sense that it continues after bodily death. After all, our individual spirit was somehow united with our body before birth. Where did it come from? Where does it go? We cannot measure, see, or make a spirit. It comes from outside our world of time and space.

At Death—Hades or Heaven?

Unlike our material world, the spiritual realm is not constrained by time and space. When we die, our spirit departs from our material body to one of two spiritual realms: Hades (not hell—see pages 20–24) or heaven. Our destiny depends on:

> Our love-relationship with God, as
> demonstrated by our acceptance
> or rejection of Jesus Christ as Lord
> and Savior (John 14:6).

God provided Himself as the ultimate sacrifice by coming to earth as Jesus. Not accepting this free gift is "thumbing our nose at God." Those who embrace Jesus go to heaven (John 5:24); others wait in Hades for the judgment at the white throne (Matthew 13:24-30,36-43).

The Sequence of Events After Death*

The following events take place after physical death (see pages 18–25):

1. The spirits of people who accept God's love through Jesus Christ go to heaven.

2. Those who do not accept Jesus Christ go to Hades to await judgment.

3. Jesus returns to the earth in glory.

4. The living accepters of Jesus are "caught up" (raptured) without dying.

5. A period of great tribulation comes for the people remaining on earth.

6. Jesus and the martyred saints rule on earth for 1000 years.

7. Satan is defeated and cast into hell (Gehenna—the final doom).

8. People's spirits are reunited with their bodies. The accepters of Jesus go to the new earth. Others face the judgment at the white throne, and most are cast into hell.

*Note: *Some theologians and denominations disagree over the timing and sequence of events. There is adequate biblical support for differing views in this area.*

The Bible on Eternal Life

The Bible frequently speaks of life after death. It says everyone will live forever somewhere—either in heaven or in hell. A few references are:

Matthew 25:41-46; 2 Thessalonians 1:8,9; and Revelation 14:9-11.

The Idea of Eternal Existence Is Logical

Based on previous evidence, let's first assume that God must exist. If God exists and has created all things including humans—

Why would He create everything for no purpose?

God is eternal. Therefore God's purpose must also be eternal (Ephesians 3:11). If humans are nothing more than matter—to be born, to live, and to then pass out of being, their existence serves no purpose whatsoever for an eternal God. On the other hand, if human beings are created to have eternal fellowship with God (Revelation 22), and since we know without doubt that the human body dies, it follows that something—namely, the spirit—must exist eternally for some purpose. The Bible makes that purpose clear: to worship and enjoy a relationship with God forever (Revelation 21:3,4).

Paranormal Evidence Supports the Existence of Eternity

The Bible strictly prohibits consulting psychics, fortune-tellers, mediums, and so on because they draw people away from God (Leviticus 19:31). *No occult practice has ever consistently foretold the future* (otherwise gambling would not exist). But there are quite a few objectively documented cases that indicate spirits exist that can reveal *past* events to people. In some cases people with so-called "psychic gifts" have led police to murder scenes. In other cases, people in apparent "near-death" states have accurately described events they could not otherwise have known about (see pages 42,43). In general, no one has been able to refute claims about the spiritual nature of these surprising events. Consequently, the occurrence of such events leads us to conclude there are spirits outside of our normal existence in time and space, just as the Bible often indicates. The existence of spirits implies the existence of an eternal realm.[2]

The Bible Reveals Eternity

For many people, the most compelling evidence for eternity and eternal life comes from the Bible. As noted earlier (see pages 6–9), we should regard the Bible as the ultimate authority on questions of eternity and life after death. Given that the Bible is accurate in hundreds of historical prophecies, we have every reason to believe that the Bible is also correct concerning future events—including eternal life. The Bible mentions eternity in relation to God (Deuteronomy 33:27) and human beings (Romans 6:23; 1 John 5:11). Many times the Bible specifically states the promise of eternal life for all who accept Jesus (for example, in John 3:16 and Titus 1:2-4). Those people who are separated from God by their refusal to accept Jesus will also face *eternal* separation from God— the "second death"—in Gehenna-hell, which is prepared for Satan (Matthew 25:41; Revelation 20:14,15; 21:8).

What Is the Purpose of Plants and Animals?

God's purpose involves human beings. So everything else on earth may have been created to support the ultimate purpose of human survival. Even what we sometimes perceive as "pests" (for example, bees) have an ultimate purpose—pollinating plants to bear fruit that humans can consume. Sometimes it is hard to understand the benefit of certain species, but eventually we will come to understand.

Life After Death According to the Bible

Test *all* claims made about life after death, because many people attempt to build doctrine on fanciful beliefs or try to make the Bible say something it doesn't. Hold onto only the truth (1 Thessalonians 5:21).

According to the Scriptures, different people have different experiences and go to different places after they die. The Bible gives us the following information about life after death.

When People Die

The Bible distinguishes the body from the spirit (or soul) in many places. It also states that the spirit leaves the body and goes somewhere upon death. The martyr Stephen gave up his spirit when he died (Acts 7:59), and Jesus gave up His spirit upon death (Matthew 27:50).

People Who Have Accepted Jesus

Those people who have, on earth, sincerely accepted Jesus as their personal Lord and Savior will be immediately transported to heaven, the abode of God. The body remains on earth to decay, but the spirit—the *real* person—goes to heaven. It's clear that heaven is a place where spirits exist, since they are sent *from* heaven (Luke 3:21,22; 1 Peter 1:12). The immediate transit of the spirit is apparent from the statement of Jesus to the thief on the cross: "Today you will be with me in paradise" (Luke 23:43—note: Paradise was the form of heaven recognized by the Jews of that time). Likewise, Paul said to be away from the body is to be at home with the Lord (2 Corinthians 5:8).

Do only those who accept Jesus go to heaven? Jesus' words in the Bible are very clear on that point: "*I am the way,* the truth and the life. *No one* comes to the Father except by me" (John 14:6, emphasis added). This is further clarified by Jesus' statement that the only way to the kingdom of God is by being "born again" (John 3:3).

> People who do not accept Jesus go immediately to *Hades* upon death—Hades is *not* hell.

Hades (*Sheol* in the Old Testament) is the "place of the spirits of the dead" (see page 21).

People Who Have Rejected Jesus

All people who do not accept Jesus as Lord and Savior are destined to *Hades* (or *Sheol* in Hebrew) after death. This includes all "knowing" people (those who can understand the gospel) who have *not accepted* Jesus, which means they have in essence *rejected* Him. There they await the judgment at the white throne, where their actions on earth (Matthew 16:27), including possibly the degree to which they have rejected Jesus, will be evaluated.

"Un-knowers"

The Bible is silent regarding a large group of people who could be called "un-knowers"—those people who (from our human point of view) do not have the capacity to understand the gospel and who therefore (again from our standpoint) do not have the chance to accept or reject Jesus. This group would include aborted babies and other children who die before or soon after birth, the mentally incapable, and others of similar mental inability (see pages 33–36 for some considerations on their destiny).

What About Hitler?

Records indicate that Hitler was a Roman Catholic and probably had a "belief" in or at least a knowledge of Jesus. Where is Hitler?

Hitler may have had an *intellectual* belief or knowledge that Jesus existed. So do demons (Matthew 9:29). But there is no evidence he ever truly accepted Jesus as his *Lord* (certainly demons don't). Therefore, Hitler would be in Hades awaiting a presumably severe judgment.

Spiritual Places*

Heaven

Most cultures and religions have a belief in some kind of heaven or paradise. The Bible describes heaven as the abode of God (Genesis 28:17; Matthew 5:34), where angels also live and serve Him (Genesis 28:12; Matthew 22:30; Revelation 5:11). Heaven is also the destination of the souls of people who have believed in and accepted Jesus Christ on earth (John 3:3). In this age, those people who have truly accepted Jesus go to heaven immediately upon death (2 Corinthians 5:8).

It seems that human souls were not permitted into heaven *until Jesus took away sin by His death on the cross and ascended into heaven.* When Jesus was on earth, He stated that no one had (yet) entered heaven (John 3:13). We also know that even the righteous people of the Old Testament went to Sheol—where they would not be left (abandoned) eternally, but would be taken to God (Psalm 16:10; 49:15; 73:24).[3]

Many people believe that the spirits of the Old Testament righteous were taken to heaven by Jesus after the crucifixion. Some have traditionally thought that Jesus Himself descended to Hades before His resurrection to lead those righteous people out, up to heaven (1 Peter 3:18-20; 4:6).[4] But entrance into heaven always requires accepting Jesus. Even for the Old Testament believers, righteousness came through faith in God's promise of a perfect sacrifice to come: a Messiah, Jesus (see *How Do We Know Jesus is God?* in the *Examine the Evidence* series). And it was Jesus who described heaven as an incredibly wonderful place (Matthew 13:44-46).

Sheol or Hades

The souls of those people who have not accepted Jesus Christ as Lord and Savior are transported to *Sheol* (the Hebrew Old Testament term), which is the same place as *Hades* (the Greek New Testament term). *Sheol* literally means "the place of the dead." Specifically, it is a "prison" where souls await the final judgment at the white throne. It is *not* "purgatory" (see page 23).[4,5]

Before Jesus, everyone went to Sheol (Hades) at death. In the story of the rich man and the beggar Lazarus (Luke 16:19-31), Jesus described Lazarus as being comforted at Abraham's side ("Abraham's bosom"—

*See chart on pages 22,23

called "paradise" by the Jews of Jesus' time), and the evil rich man as being in a "place of torment"—and indicated that their destination was determined by their actions on earth. (Some people have suggested that there are also "intermediate" places in Sheol.)[4]

From this account in Luke and from other New Testament references to it by Jesus, Hades seems to be a place of torment *for those who are able to choose the gift of God's Son but don't*. Their decision would eventually lead to eternal horror in hell.

However, we should remember that Jesus' words were directed *to those who could hear Him and who had the capability to understand the message*. What about those who, from our viewpoint, can't hear, understand, or in any way grasp Jesus' message (for example, aborted babies—see pages 33–36)? It would seem to be both sheer speculation and illogical to think that He was talking at that time to aborted babies and other people incapable of understanding. We should not go beyond what Jesus said and assume an absolute message about the many unfortunate people who cannot hear or understand His message. Again, the Bible is silent on this issue. But for those *capable* of understanding the message, going to Hades because of their rejection of Jesus seals their final doom in hell (see pages 34–36 for a discussion of God's final judgment).

Abraham's Bosom

Does "paradise"—"Abraham's bosom"—still exist? Many people believe it does not, since the righteous people of the Old Testament have been taken to heaven by Jesus (see page 20). Others have suggested that it still does exist, and that it is a waiting place for the spirits of the "unknowers" (see pages 18,19,33–36)—who will be given a *"first chance"* there to accept Jesus.

Tartarus

Peter used this Greek word—translated "hell" in several Bible versions—to describe the "gloomy dungeons" to which God consigned angels who sinned (2 Peter 2:4). It is not clear whether this place is part of Hades (as many scholars believe is implied by the words "gloomy dungeons") or is separate from it. The Bible also does not say whether there are any human spirits in Tartarus.

What Happens After Death?

Heaven—
a spiritual abode with God

The Spirit Leaves the Body

Those who have accepted Jesus

Those who reject Jesus

"Un-knowers of Jesus (?)

SOMETIME IN THE FUTURE

The spirit is reunited with the body

New Heaven

New Earth

Those who accepted Jesus

The Great Tribulation

The 1000-Year Reign of Christ

The Judgment at the White Throne

Souls of people who have not accepted Christ await the burial for the judgement

Sheol-Hades
(a place of the spirits of the dead)

Tartarus?

Note: While the events here are accepted by virtually all Bible-based denominations, some differ on the timing or manner presented here. See pages 18–21,24,25 for descriptions and explanations.

Great Chasm

Place of Comfort—"Abraham's Bosom" (if still in existence)

The faithful people of the Old Testament and (perhaps) "Un-knowers" of Jesus

The spirit is reunited with the body

Those who did not accept Jesus

Gehenna (Hell, the Lake of Fire)

Future Places of the Afterlife

The New Heaven and the New Earth

The current heaven and earth will pass away (Matthew 24:35; 2 Peter 3:7,12,13) and will be replaced with a new heaven and new earth (Revelation 21:1). Why will God do this?

Consider that God created the first heaven and earth as part of His desire to have fellowship with human beings (Genesis 3:8-24). Human beings chose to disobey God instead of keeping a relationship with Him. Thus sin separated them from God. God's infinite wisdom and love prompted the provision of a Savior (Jesus) to allow human beings to *reselect* Him and to *be forgiven*. The acceptance of Jesus as Lord and Savior allows human beings to exist eternally with God again.

The earth as it exists today is greatly stained by sin. The new earth—free from sin—is necessary to perfect God's intentions. As the Bible states, God will interact with humans in the new earth, just as He intended to originally in the garden of Eden (Revelation 21:3; 22:3-5).

Gehenna

Gehenna is hell—the place of eternal torment for those whose names are not recorded in God's "book of life." Gehenna differs from Hades in that Hades is *temporary*, for *souls only*, while Gehenna is a place of *eternal* condemnation after the soul has been reunited *with the body* (John 5:28,29; Revelation 20:10-15). Jesus used the word "Gehenna" when referring to the eternal hell. Gehenna was a horrifying garbage dump near Jerusalem where human flesh—that of the most vile criminals—was burned in continual flames; a foul odor permeated the area. By using Gehenna as a vivid description from real life, Jesus made the terrifying prospect of eternal hell real to those who listened.

Events Related to the Afterlife

The Rapture

At some point in the future, God will "take up" ("rapture") the church. All true Christians will "meet the Lord in the air" (1 Thessalonians 4:17), which will preclude death for them. Many say that the rapture will be a precursor to the great tribulation. Others suggest that the rapture will be during or after the tribulation, depending on their view of end-time events.

The Great Tribulation

Before the end of the world as we know it, there will be a time of great suffering (Matthew 24:6-14). Some scholars estimate that it will last seven years. During that time, the earth will be overwhelmed with plagues, earthquakes, wars, and other kinds of troubles.

The Thousand-Year Reign (the Millennium)

The term "millennium" refers to a 1000-year peaceful reign of Christ on earth (Revelation 20:6). There are three primary views of the millennium: 1) *Amillennial*—the millennium is figurative, and we have been living in it since the destruction of the Jewish temple in A.D. 70; 2) *Postmillennial*—the millennium has already occurred and has been completed; and 3) *Premillennial*—the millennium is literal and has yet to take place. This is the most widely accepted view, although the others have some merits.

The Judgment at the White Throne

The spirits in Hades will be reunited with their bodies to face the judgment at the white throne, where they will be evaluated for their actions—most importantly, whether they have accepted Jesus Christ as Lord and Savior (Revelation 13:8; 20:11-15). The evil ones, those convicted of blasphemy of the Holy Spirit (that is, continually rejecting the Holy Spirit's prompting to follow Jesus) will go to Gehenna (hell). People who accepted Jesus will be resurrected with glorified bodies to dwell on an incredible new earth and in the new Jerusalem (Revelation 21).

One Person's Journey Through Death

An Imaginary Conception of Hades Based on the Bible's Teaching

Fred pondered John's comments from moments ago on the golf course. Today John seemed especially filled with energy and happiness as he raved about the love of Jesus for the "umpty-umpth" time. Ten years and thousands of holes of golf with John had not changed Fred's skepticism. Then he stepped on the gas—tonight was poker night.

Fred smiled wryly and thought, *John's got his little happiness crutch with the Jesus thing, but I've got his money,* as he shook the four quarters in his hand—the usual prize for a four-hole win. He paused again for a second and wondered why John seemed so obsessed with Jesus. Then, coming back to his senses as he drove out of the parking lot, he laughed and vowed again never to be obsessed with anyone. No, his motto was "live for today."

Suddenly, from nowhere—a truck . . . screeeeeeech . . . baaaaam! Glass shattering, steel scraping . . . folding like cardboard . . . fire, searing heat . . . breath squeezed out. . . . Fred blacked out.

A New World

Instantaneously, Fred felt weightless—tenuous . . . there was a foreboding impression of total darkness. There was no question what had happened. He knew he was dead. But what was this strange new sensation of existence? Where was he? What was going on? Looking around, Fred caught glimpses of wisps of beings moving to and fro. No bodies—just impressions of people. Yet he could distinguish individuals. Looking down, he realized he also had no body. Nothing. And there was an overpowering air of gloom.

"Welcome to Hades," boomed a voice he recognized—that of his old poker buddy, Jim—who had died a year ago of cancer. They'd had many laughs over the years about John's "Jesus obsession" as they'd pounded down beers over piles of poker chips. But Jim's words were not in the same fun-loving spirit he remembered on earth. They had the cutting edge of deep pain.

"What's this all about?" asked Fred.

"You're here until the *day*," said Jim. "It's the day we line up for our final sentence."

Jim sped off as if to get somewhere. As Fred continued to watch, beings moved quickly about, seemingly going somewhere and nowhere at the same time. Quickly moving around like the others, Fred found the boundaries of his area. Beyond those boundaries was nothing that he could perceive, try as he might. One thing became obvious, though. Fred was locked in some kind of a prison. Darkness was all around, and there was no way to escape. All he could do was wait.

The Day

Without any warning, a magnet-like force grabbed Fred, pulling him into a line of spirit people, where he suddenly found himself clothed with a new body. Frozen with anticipation, Fred was slowly pushed toward an enormous white throne surmounted by an incredible, piercing glow of pure white light. Finally faced with the blinding glow, Fred saw that a book was opened—and a voice boomed, "What did you do with My gift—the precious life of My Son Jesus?" He had no answer. The book was slammed shut. A deafening silence.

Jerked into pitch-black darkness, Fred tumbled. Scorching, unbearable heat enveloped his entire being. Like molten sulfur, it seemed to cling to his flesh, not burning it . . . and never going out. Screams of others. Weeping. Gnashing of teeth . . . forever. And ever.

27

Another Person's Journey Through Death

An Imaginary Conception of Heaven Based on the Bible's Teaching

John left the course with a feeling of joy and questioning. For years he had hoped Fred would consider Jesus, and today he had seemed more receptive than ever. John knew Fred had other priorities and hoped he would "get the message" before it was too late. He smiled, thinking the four holes he had just lost on the golf course might be an inexpensive investment in Fred's eternal life.

John had experienced sudden headaches for the past few weeks, and one seemed to be starting as he walked across the parking lot. He'd ask his doctor about the pain at his annual physical next week.

Suddenly, a fierce pain shot through John's head—and his last thought was that his body was crumpling to the ground. John had had a fatal stroke from a brain aneurysm.

A New World

An intense yet gentle light glowed in the distance. John wondered what had happened. Somehow he sensed impressions of thousands of people. All of them were without bodies, yet each had a distinctive look and personality. He looked down—his body was also gone. An immense feeling of peace, love, and total contentment, such as he had never experienced or even imagined before, seemed to pierce through his entire being. Faces of others, people he had never known, expressed incredible joy, love, and caring. Around everyone was an intense light. It filled everything and literally took away all darkness, both day and night. All people were bathed in its glow. Only love seemed to exist. Sadness, sickness, and problems were a thing of the past. People said that the Spirit of God was within them.

Finally he saw it—the throne of God. Such splendor . . . he could not possibly describe it. Spectacular light. Precious gems. Crystal. Transparent gold. Now he understood the difficulty of describing heaven. No earthly words could have expressed what he was experiencing.

The Day

Time stood still. Suddenly, John was reunited with a body. Not an old, aged body, but a new one, perfect in every way. A trumpet sounded, and everyone was lined up before the throne of light. It was an awards ceremony! People were given rewards based on how they had used their talents and how they lived out their love for Jesus. John received crowns of love for many of his deeds, including his efforts to minister to Fred. It was a celebration to end all celebrations. Incredible delight and happiness filled everyone, as songs of joy and praise echoed throughout heaven.

Eternity

A city formed around John and those who were with him. It was like nothing ever seen on earth. The city was 1400 miles wide by 1400 miles long and extended 1400 miles into the sky. It was decorated with perfect jewels and precious metals. The foundation was diamond and was decorated with precious stones. The streets were paved with gold refined so perfectly that it was clear. There was neither sun nor moon, because the glory of God shone like light—day and night for all eternity. And there was no sadness, no weeping, no pain. A river of life flowed through the city, and at that river there was a tree of life yielding wonderful fruit forever. All the city was filled to overflowing with tremendous joy and peace. All needs were met. All desires were realized. The pain and trouble of the earth melted away into the past.

What Heaven Is Like

Virtually all cultures have some concept of heaven. Yet none of these concepts is supported by the evidence in the way the Bible is (see pages 6–9).

Heaven Described

Heaven is beyond imagining—beyond all description. Jesus proclaimed that heaven would be worth trading everything for (Matthew 13:44-46). But the most complete description of heaven is in Revelation. Keep in mind that John, the author of Revelation, was shown many things that are totally unlike anything here on earth. Consequently, he had to express heaven's beauty in terms of the earthly beauty that was familiar to him and his readers.

What Does Heaven Look Like?

The throne: God is on it. It has the appearance of jasper* and carnelian. There are blazes of lightning and thunder.

The rainbow around the throne: "like an emerald" (Revelation 4:3).

The 24 elders around the throne: They are dressed in white with crowns on their heads. Perhaps they are the leaders of the 12 tribes of Israel and the 12 apostles.

The sea of glass**: In front of the throne—"like crystal."

The glorious creatures: Four of them surround the throne. Each has six wings and many eyes covering them. They have the heads of a lion, an ox, a man, and an eagle.***

What Do We Do in Heaven?

Worship: It will be a great and everlasting spiritual thrill to worship the one almighty God in heaven.

Enjoy God: For the first time since Adam, God will truly exist with humankind (Revelation 21:4).

Enjoy other people: Believers will live with other believers, including family and friends.

Have no sorrow, ever: No more death, no more mourning, no more sadness—forever.

Be filled with delight: Incredible heavenly golf courses? Symphonies beyond description? We can only imagine it in terms of the best of earth. God promises us eternal pleasure (Psalm 16:11).

(See Revelation 4,20,21)

* Jasper, at the time of Christ, was the name for diamond.
** Perfectly refined gold is clear like glass.
*** Lion=king, ox=slave, man=man, eagle=God. These are the primary roles of Jesus that are reflected in the Gospels.

While we won't be able to experience or even truly imagine the wonder of heaven until we arrive, we can trust the words of Jesus that heaven is worth more than anything (Matthew 13:44-46).

Heaven and Earth Today— A New Heaven and Earth Tomorrow

Heaven today is the abode of God, the spirits of people who have accepted Jesus, and the angels that serve God. Only *spirits* now exist in heaven—spirits without bodies. After the second coming of Jesus, the spirits of people in heaven will be reunited with their new glorified bodies (2 Corinthians 5:4,5; Revelation 20:4), and God's people will enjoy a new, "heavenly" earth with no more tears, suffering, or death (Revelation 21:4).

The Bible makes a distinction between the heaven of today—and the new heaven and the new earth to come (Revelation 21:1). Earth is for bodies united with spirits. Heaven is for spirits only. *Everyone* will be united for eternity with a body—whether a glorious, indestructible one in heaven, or one subject to eternal torment in hell. And God will reside with believers for eternity on the new earth (Revelation 21:3).

The new earth, specifically the holy city, the new Jerusalem, is described in glorious terms. It will shine in the brilliance of the light emanating from God Himself (Revelation 21:11). It will have walls of jasper—diamond (21:18), streets of pure gold (transparent), and gates of pearl (21:21). Very significantly, it will contain the "tree of life" mentioned at the beginning, at the time of the great separation of mankind from God (Genesis 3:22,23). There will no longer be any curse against man or upon the earth (Revelation 22:3). And, the throne of God will be the throne of both God and Jesus, the Lamb (the remover of the curse through His sacrifice on the cross—see 22:1).

What Hell Is Like

Hell (Gehenna) is also beyond description, and there is no place on earth that compares to it. Jesus used the word "Gehenna" because it was the most relevant description to the Jews of His time.

The Horror of Hell

Gehenna is an actual place in the Hinnom Valley just southwest of Jerusalem. Solomon, in his later years, turned the valley from a natural paradise into a place where the idols of his wives' pagan gods were worshipped. Infants were sacrificed into terrifying flames. The valley later became the city cesspool where refuse, dead animals, and bodies of criminals were dumped and burned. Worms ate into dead flesh until they were consumed by the blaze. The fires never ceased. The foul stench never stopped. To the Jews, Gehenna was absolute hell.

The Bible describes hell several times as a place where "fires never cease" (for example, in Mark 9:43), where a lake of fire burns with sulfur (Revelation 19:20), and where worms never die (Mark 9:47,48).

The darkness of hell is complete. Since the only light at the end of time, in heaven, will be from God and Jesus (Revelation 21:23-25; 22:5), hell will be eternal darkness—a place where everyone and everything is separated from God forever (Matthew 8:12; 22:13; 25:30).

Jesus used the earthly horror of Gehenna to describe the horror of hell. Jesus never minced words. He was direct. Hell is horrible. Jesus described hell several times as the place where there will be "weeping and gnashing of teeth" (Matthew 8:12; 22:13; 24:51; 25:30).

> While it is difficult to know exactly what hell is, we can be certain it is a terrible place that everyone would want to avoid.

What Happens to Aborted Babies?

The Bible clearly states Jesus Christ is the only way to heaven and that *no one* comes to the Father except through Him (John 14:6). This may be difficult to accept for some people who are resistant to accepting Jesus as both Lord and Savior.

What about aborted babies, severely mentally impaired people, young children, and others who do not have the opportunity to hear (or understand) the gospel of Jesus? Does the Bible imply that they go to Gehenna (hell)?

What the Bible Says

We must gain understanding from the Bible based on *what it actually says*, without reading words or opinions into it. While it is clear that Jesus is the *only* way to heaven, it is also clear God will not condemn anyone for failing to respond to a message he has not heard. Consider the faithful people of the Old Testament who looked forward to a Messiah, but didn't know Jesus. Were Noah, Moses, Abraham, and David condemned to hell? No! In fact, the Bible teaches that Abraham was saved—made righteous—by believing God about what God revealed to him, as was David (Romans 4:5-8; Galatians 3:6-9).

The Bible Says God Is Just

The evidence that supports the Bible and the words of Jesus—and their many statements about an afterlife—is the strongest ground for confidence in the existence of life after death. However, justice in itself is also a reason for believing in an afterlife. Since God's justice on earth now often seems to us to be hidden or not complete, or even "too late" (Ecclesiastes 8:14; Habakkuk 1:3), God must have a method to reveal and apply perfect justice. Life after death makes a place for complete justice, because God's justness will certainly be revealed in all its perfection, magnificence, and holiness in the afterlife (Psalm 9:7,8). Since God will judge all people according to their actions (Matthew 16:27) and their thoughts (Romans 2:16), an aborted baby will not be judged in the same way as a "Jesus-mocking" murderer.[3]

The Bible Says We Will Be Judged Fairly

It stands to reason that those people, such as aborted babies, who do not have the full message of the gospel of Jesus Christ will not be judged in the same way as those who do. The Bible declares this to be so (Romans 2:12-14). Those who hear about Jesus but do not accept Him will be judged differently than those who never hear this message. We will all be judged according to the light we receive.

However, any person who has ever lived has received *some* light from God, because all people have a "voice" within them—the conscience. This voice says that some things are right and good, and other things are wrong and bad. The Bible indicates that this "law" inside of people is a revelation of the existence of the God who created the conscience (Romans 2:12-16; also 1:18-20). But those people who *in spite of this and in spite of hearing about Jesus* (and the Holy Spirit prompts all such people—see John 16:7-11) still reject His sacrifice—thus rejecting God's love and effectively thumbing their noses at God *forever*—will surely be judged more harshly. This is the one unforgivable sin: blasphemy of the Holy Spirit (Matthew 12:31,32).

Will All People Who Go to Hades and Appear at the White Throne Be Condemned to Hell?

At the white throne judgment, the "book of life" will be opened, and those people whose names are not found in the book will be thrown into the lake of fire (Revelation 20:12-15). It is likely that the book of life originally contained the names of all people, but that the names of those people who reject Jesus, the perfect Lamb who died for the sins of the whole world, are later "blotted out" (Exodus 32:32,33; Psalm 69:28; Revelation 3:5; 13:8; 17:8).[6]

What does this have to do with the "un-knowers"—aborted babies and others who (to the extent of our knowledge) would not have the capacity while on earth to understand the Spirit's prompting about Jesus—and therefore would not have the capacity to reject Him? It would mean that they could go to eternal paradise, if somehow in Hades they are given a chance to accept Jesus. This would not be a "second chance" for them, since they would never have had a "first chance."

However, many people also see the Scriptures clearly indicating that the actions, words, and thoughts done *"in the body"* (on the earth), above all choosing or rejecting Jesus, will be the basis of judgment in the afterlife (Matthew 25:31-46; 2 Corinthians 5:10). In other words, the judgment at the white throne will not be an *investigation*, but rather a *declaration* based upon what God already knows about people—which is *absolutely everything* (Hebrews 4:13).[3] Because human beings do not know everything and are simply not capable of judging other humans' spiritual capacity in this life, there remains a "gray area" of uncertainty for us about the "un-knowers."

One thing is certain: If the evidence can be accepted that the Bible is a miraculous text from beyond time and space, unique in its prophetic accuracy and its authority about life after death, then everything it says about God can also be accepted, because it is "from God" (see pages 6,7). The Bible says God knows everything about human beings (Hebrews 4:13), and that He is perfect in His judgments, His holiness, and His love.[3] Since He is perfect, He can be trusted in the things the Bible does not say anything about—such as the destiny of aborted babies, children, the severely mentally handicapped, and others who (from the human point of view) are not capable of hearing the gospel.

Ultimately, we don't know why the Bible does not reveal more about life after death. Perhaps God wants to emphasize the necessity of relating to Him in faith (Hebrews 11:6). Perhaps the reality of heaven is so inconceivably great (in comparison to what we can know and understand on earth) that it simply cannot be communicated to us in this life. Perhaps He wants us to keep going back to the Bible so we can know Him better and learn to trust Him more for who He is. But we do know this—after we die, He will judge each of us with the question, "What did you do with My gift—the precious life of My Son Jesus?"

Angels and Demons

Angels are usually thought of as "fantasy" creatures that exist to help everyone. People's images of them often include "cupids," attractive flying females with wings, and any number of cute little ornaments. Demons (and devils) are often thought of in an opposite vein of fantasy. They are usually red, cute, mean-looking, and carry a pitchfork. Unfortunately, these images undermine the reality of angels and demons.

Both angels and demons are real. They exist in the spiritual realm beyond time and space. The Bible often refers to them (about 400 times!). Again, since we can be very confident in the Bible's accuracy in predicting the future (see pages 6–9), we can also trust it on difficult-to-comprehend issues such as the nature of angels and demons.

Angels

Angels can be grouped into two categories: 1) those who are *servants of God* (the most common description in the Bible) and 2) "fallen" angels—those who *followed Satan* when his pride led him to attempt to be like God and, consequently, to be banished from God. It is these banished angels whom many scholars believe to be the demons the Bible speaks of, and who will be referred to here by that term. The angels discussed here are only those angels who are servants of God.

Are angels cute and chubby—like those little ornaments? Only if you can envision cute little angels slaughtering hundreds of thousands of people in a short period of time. Angels carry out such judgments because they are called upon to execute God's will, which has included the killing of thousands of people during a plague in Israel (2 Samuel 24:15-17) and the slaughter of 185,000 Assyrians in one night (2 Kings 19:35). Yet these episodes pale in comparison to the events at the end of time, when angels will kill one-third of all humans (Revelation 9:15). The angel Michael is thought to be the leader of the military angels (Daniel 10:10-21; Revelation 12:7).

God also uses angels for many peaceful purposes. The word "angel" literally means *messenger*. Gabriel is the Bible's renowned "angel of news," responsible for foretelling 1) the future of Israel to Daniel (Daniel 8:16-26); 2) the exact day that the Messiah would present Himself (Daniel 9:21-27); 3) the birth of John the Baptist (Luke 1:19); and 4) the coming of Jesus (Luke 1:26).

In heaven, we will coexist with the angels, yet we will be regarded as "higher" than angels in God's eyes. In fact, believers will actually judge angels (1 Corinthians 6:3).

Demons

The Bible refers to demons as real beings and mentions them well over 100 times. Demons are spirit-based creatures that exist to undermine the work of God. They follow Satan (Matthew 25:41). As mentioned earlier, many students of the Bible believe that demons are the "fallen" angels that joined Satan after his pride separated him from God (Isaiah 14:12-15).

Demons exist eternally. They believe that Jesus is the Son of God (Matthew 8:29; Mark 1:23,24), yet nonetheless they work with Satan to battle against righteousness (Ephesians 6:12). They can affect or even possess humans (Matthew 12:43-45).

Exposing Myths About Angels

1. *People do not become angels.* It's a popular belief, but there is no evidence to support it. The Bible states that people are beneath angels today (Psalm 8:5) and will be above them in heaven (1 Corinthians 6:3).

2. *Angels are personal beings.* They have emotions (Hebrew 12:20), intelligence (2 Samuel 14:20), and morality (Revelation 22:8,9).

3. *Angels are spirits that can take on the appearance of humans.* At times they have appeared indistinguishable from humans (Genesis 19:1-17; Hebrews 13:2).

4. *Angels are immortal.* They were among God's first created beings and do not die (Luke 20:36).

5. *Angels are intelligent and powerful.* They have existed for a long time and can use their experience to predict human behavior (as can demons). God has used them to decimate powerful armies.

"Purgatory" and "Soul Sleep"

Purgatory?

The Roman Catholic Church teaches that baptized souls who fall short of immediate entrance to heaven (which is virtually everyone) and who are not evil enough for hell go to a place called "purgatory" at death. There, souls are punished for insufficient penitence of sins committed after baptism. When the debt is fully paid, they have then been completely "purged" (purified—hence the word "purgatory") and are released into heaven. This tradition was formalized into doctrine by the Latin Catholic church in the eleventh century, and the doctrine was given its final shape at the Council of Trent (1545–63).[4]

There is absolutely no biblical basis for the punishment of believers in some type of purgatory. The Bible says the opposite—that there is no condemnation for those in Christ Jesus (Romans 8:1). The idea of purgatory is not the same as Hades, which is a place of the dead, a prison, where nonbelievers await the judgment at the white throne. Purgatory is like a temporary hell, where believers are harshly punished. It contradicts the New Testament's teaching of the complete redemption of believers by God's grace alone (Romans 3:22,23; Ephesians 2:8; 2 Timothy 1:9).

The usual defense of the idea of purgatory is found deep in Roman Catholic tradition, dating back to the birth of the concept in the sixth century under Pope Gregory I. There are *no scriptural texts that support the idea of purgatory*, but the Catholic Church claims 2 Maccabees 12:43-46 as a "proof text." However, 2 Maccabees is not a part of holy Scripture—it is part of a collection of additional writings called the Apocrypha. The Apocrypha was *never* considered Scripture by the early Jews and Christians, by the church, or by Jesus Himself. It was "deuterocanonized" (given a secondary position as inspired Scripture) in the sixteenth century by the Catholic Church.[7]

Soul Sleep?

Some religious organizations teach that the soul goes into a period of sleep until reunited with the body at the resurrection (referred to as "soul sleep"). Often the basis for this theory is the belief that man is no different from animals because all were made when God breathed life into them. The Scriptures clearly indicate many differences between humans and animals, though, including where the spirit goes upon death (Ecclesiastes 3:21). More importantly, there are scriptural references to people's experience as that of being translated at death from the bodily state to a spiritual state in Hades or heaven (Psalm 16:10,11; Luke 16:22; Acts 2:25-31).

Near-Death Experiences

A Near-Death Experience (NDE) is a seemingly spiritual phenomenon that some people experience upon "clinical" death. It generally involves some or all of the following impressions:

- Hearing a pronouncement of death
- A feeling of peace and contentment
- A feeling of darkness, of being in a tunnel or a void
- Separation from the body

- Meeting others who have died
- Experiencing a "life review"
- Coming back, often reluctantly
- A changed view of life and death

Many near-death experiences have been recorded. They are not a new phenomenon. NDE ideas go back as far as Zoroaster (625 B.C.), Plato (427 B.C.) and Buddha (560 B.C.). A Gallup poll reports that more than *20 million* Americans indicate they have had a near-death experience.[8] The accounts are amazing, seemingly far beyond mere coincidence. Some people see and hear things that they could not possibly have witnessed—since their bodies remained on the operating table—such as discussions in other rooms and even details of events involving family members after they left the hospital. There is frequently independent corroboration of the evidence by others. There is no doubt that people have near-death experiences. The real issue is, *What do they mean?*

Do NDEs Prove Life After Death?

No. How could they? We are still trying to determine when physical death actually occurs. We once thought death came upon cessation of the heartbeat. Electronic shock equipment changed that, as we could bring silent hearts back to life. Then we redefined death as "absence of brain activity." Now, that too is in question. NDEs show us there can definitely be a state of consciousness at the time when we are classified as "dead."

That surviving state of consciousness can be viewed as supporting the Bible's many claims about "everlasting life." But it is the usual conclusions about near-death experiences that should be questioned. Fascinating questions include, How do dead people get information about conversations in other rooms or miles away? How do they "see" colors and styles of clothing?

Consider the existence of spirits (which is a basic teaching of the Bible). No one but God can foretell the future (Isaiah 46:10). But of course spirits—including Satan—can know the past and present. We might then reckon that evil spirits would often use near-death experiences to lure people into a worldview that is against the Bible. And that is in fact the case. Many, though certainly not all, people involved in NDE research are in the occult or are otherwise at odds with biblical teaching.*

*Dr. Michael Sabom, a cardiologist, is one of the few reliable researchers.[2]

Did the Apostle Paul Have an NDE?

Paul tells about the experience of a "man" (believed to be Paul) who was transported to the "third heaven," where he saw and experienced "inexpressible things" (2 Corinthians 12:2). Some scholars believe that this was a near-death experience, perhaps taking place at one of the times Paul was nearly killed (1 Corinthians 11:23-25).

There is not enough information to know whether this is what we would today call an NDE. What we can be certain of is that God chose to give much of His message to the world through Paul, who wrote more of the New Testament than anyone else. And it is impossible that God would allow any evil spirit to distort His message to humankind.

Facing Death

Death is the ultimately personal experience. No one knows what others have felt at death. No one really knows death—except Jesus Christ, who has overcome it.* And with the right relationship with Him and the right perspective He gives us, death should be wonderful, glorious, beyond anyone's imagination! Death is actually a gift from God.

1. Recognize the Eternal Perspective— Accept Jesus

To discover why death is a gift, we must first envision it from an eternal perspective. Death is permanent. Provided that this permanent situation is indescribable bliss, it must be an amazing adventure for those enjoying it—far better than our earthly existence. On the other hand, if eternity is uncomfortable—no, let's say *unbearable*—then death will be a horror. How do we choose?

The Bible has given us very specific evidence about heaven and hell. It also tells us how to select the one over the other. The pathway to heaven is free. It only takes 1) a commitment to move away from a prideful, self-centered view of life (and eternity) and 2) allowing ourselves to be shown the love of God by *trusting Jesus Christ to be the director of our lives*. No act, word, or thought against God is unforgivable.

Again: No sins are unforgivable—if you accept Christ (Matthew 12:31).

A relationship with God brings love to us far beyond what we could ever experience without Him. God *wants* to have a relationship with us. Yet He has also given everyone the choice to accept or reject Him. He gave the most amazing gift any human can imagine: the humiliating, painful sacrifice of His only Son, so that people could be forgiven. Even so, some people reject that sacrifice. Others accept it. Those who accept it go to the eternal paradise we call heaven.

---

* See *What Is the Proof for the Resurrection?* in the *Examine the Evidence* series.

Establishing and then solidifying a relationship with God requires only four simple steps (see page 46). Essentially, it involves believing in Jesus, accepting His sacrifice on the cross as that which takes away our sin, repenting (switching from the world's life-style to God's life-style) and expressing our new repentance, and accepting God as the director of all of our life.

2. Focus on the Benefits

The benefits of heaven are not trivial. They are enormous. No more pain, no more tears, no more sorrow—in a heavenly body that lasts forever and ever. Since no human has ever been able to put into words the benefits of heaven, we can only imagine them from the perspective of the best earth can offer. Maybe we'll hear incredible symphonies forever. Maybe we'll play golf on heavenly golf courses. Maybe we'll journey to times and places we could never dream of. Whatever your delight, it may well exist in heaven, only far greater and better. So when we face death, it's a good idea to focus on the heavenly benefits instead of the loss of earthly family and friends. Remember, if our loved ones are Christians, they will someday be joining us—forever and ever and ever. Any immediate loss, though sorrowful and hard to bear, is temporary. *Focus on the eternal.*

3. Share God's Love with Others

Sometimes dying people don't want to share anything with anyone. But when we have a relationship with God, it becomes obvious, and He wants us to show it. Suffering and pain are temporary. But God's love lasts forever. Sharing God's love reinforces it in us, and puts us at peace. Jesus said:

"Do not let your hearts be troubled. Trust in God; trust also in me. In my Father's house there are many rooms...I am going there to prepare a place for you. And...I will come again and take you to be with me that you also may be where I am" (John 14:1-3).

Common Questions

Wouldn't a Loving God Allow Good People into Heaven?

Many people believe that living a good life and being kind to others is the way to heaven. The Bible says that the only way to heaven is through a relationship with Jesus Christ (John 14:6). So will loving and "good" people who don't accept Jesus go to Gehenna (hell)? Not if they are *perfectly* loving and good. On the other hand, do truly "good" people reject the love of someone who died for them?

God would allow perfectly good people into heaven. But His standard is perfection (Matthew 5:48). That means *any* sin of either mind or body (Matthew 5:28) would keep us from that perfection. What looks like a minor sin to us is still important to God (Romans 3:9-23; James 2:10). Hence, *everyone* is imperfect. But God provided Jesus as a perfect sacrifice. Not accepting God's gift of love and forgiveness through Jesus, despite the Holy Spirit's prompting, is unforgivable (Mark 3:29).

How Can We Ensure the Right Relationship So We Can Go to Heaven?

When Jesus said not all who use His name will enter heaven (Matthew 7:21-23), He was referring to people who think using Christ's name along with rules and rituals is the key to heaven. A *relationship* with God is not based on rituals and rules. It's based on grace, forgiveness, and on having the right standing with Him through Jesus Christ.

How to Have a Personal Relationship with God

1. **B***elieve that God exists* and that He came to earth in the human form of Jesus Christ (John 3:16; Romans 10:9).

2. **A***ccept God's free forgiveness of sins* through the death and resurrection of Jesus Christ (Ephesians 1:7,8; 2:8-10).

3. **S***witch to God's plan* for your life (1 Peter 1:21-23; Ephesians 2:1-5).

4. **E***xpress desire for Christ to be director of your life* (Matthew 7:21-27; 1 John 4:15).

Prayer for Eternal Life with God

"Dear God, I believe You sent Your Son, Jesus, to die for my sins so I can be forgiven. I'm sorry for my sins, and I want to live the rest of my life the way You want me to. Please put Your Spirit in my life to direct me. Amen."

Then What?

People who have sincerely taken these steps automatically become members of God's family of believers. A new world of freedom and strength is available through prayer and obedience to God's will. New believers can also build their relationship with God by taking the following steps:

- Find a Bible-based church that you like and attend regularly.
- Try to set aside some time each day to pray and read the Bible.
- Locate other Christians to spend time with on a regular basis.

God's Promises to Believers

For Today

But seek first His kingdom and His righteousness, and all these things [things to satisfy all your needs] will be given to you as well.
—Matthew 6:33

For Eternity

Whoever believes in the Son has eternal life, but whoever rejects the Son will not see life, for God's wrath remains on him.
—John 3:36

Once we develop an eternal perspective, even the greatest problems on earth fade in significance.

Notes

Note: The author does not agree with *all* authors below on *all* viewpoints. Each reference has some findings worthy of consideration. ("Test everything"—1 Thessalonians 5:21).

1. Walvoord, John F., *The Prophecy Knowledge Handbook*, Wheaton, IL: Victor Books, 1990.

2. Sabom, Michael, M.D., *Light and Death*, Grand Rapids, MI: Zondervan Publishing House, 1998. [Recommended]

3. Blanchard, John, *Whatever Happened to Hell?* Darlington, Durham, England: Evangelical Press, 1993.

4. Baxter, J. Sidlow, *The Other Side of Death*, Grand Rapids, MI: Kregel, 1987.

5. Elwell, Walter A. (Editor), *Evangelical Dictionary of Theology*, Grand Rapids, MI: Baker Book House Co., 1984.

6. Thomas, Robert L., *Revelation: An Exegetical Commentary*, 2 vols., Chicago, IL: Moody Press, 1992, pp. 259–264.

7. Muncaster, Ralph O., *The Bible—Manuscript Reliability—Investigation of the Evidence*, Mission Viejo, CA: Strong Basis to Believe, 1996.

8. Abanes, Richard, *Journey into the Light*, Grand Rapids, MI: Baker Book House Co., 1996.

Bibliography

Eby, Richard E., D.O., *Caught Up into Paradise*, Old Tappan, NJ: Fleming H. Revell Company, 1978.

Encyclopedia Britannica, Chicago, IL: 1993.

Graham, Billy, *Death and the Life After*, Dallas, TX: Word Publishing, 1987.

Habermas, Gary R. and Moreland, J.P., *Immortality*, Nashville, TN: Nelson, 1992.

Hick, John, *Death and Eternal Life*, Louisville, KY: Westminster John Knox Press, 1994.

Jeffrey, Grant R., *Heaven—the Mystery of Angels*, Toronto, Ontario: Frontier Research Publications Inc., 1996.

Life Application Bible, Wheaton, IL: Tyndale House Publishers, and Grand Rapids, MI: Zondervan Publishing House, 1991.

Mc Dowell, Josh, *Handbook of Today's Religions,* San Bernardino, CA: Campus Crusade for Christ, 1983.

Mc Dowell, Josh, and Wilson, Bill, *A Ready Defense*, San Bernardino, CA: Here's Life Publishers, Inc., 1990.

Morse, Melvin, and Raymond A. Moody Jr., *Closer to the Light: Learning from Near Death Experiences,* New York: Ivy Books, 1991. [Caution]

Muncaster, Ralph O., *The Bible—Prophecy Miracles—Investigation of the Evidence*, Mission Viejo, CA: Strong Basis to Believe, 1997.

Packer, J. I., Tenney, Merrill C., and White, William Jr., *Illustrated Encyclopedia of Bible Facts*, Nashville, TN: Thomas Nelson, Inc., 1980.

Rhodes, Ron, *Angels Among Us*, Eugene, OR: Harvest House Publishers, 1994.

Ring, Dr. Kenneth, *Lessons from the Light*, Reading, MA: Perseus Books, 1998. [Caution]

Smith, F. LaGard, *The Daily Bible in Chronological Order*, Eugene, OR: Harvest House, 1984.

Youngblood, Ronald F., *New Illustrated Bible Dictionary*, Nashville, TN: Nelson, 1995.